BODY NEEDS

Vitamins and Minerals
for a Healthy Body

Angela Royston

Heinemann Library
Chicago, Illinois

Printed and bound in China by CTPS

13 12 11 10 09
10 9 8 7 6 5 4 3 2 1

Library of Congress Cataloging-in-Publication Data
Royston, Angela.
   Vitamins and minerals for a healthy body / Angela Royston.
      p. cm.
   Summary: Discusses what vitamins and minerals are, how they are digested, absorbed, and used by the body, and the role of these substances in a healthy diet.
   Includes bibliographical references and index.
   ISBN 978 1 432921 89 7 (hb)
   ISBN 978 1 432921 95 8 (pb)
   1. Vitamins in human nutrition--Juvenile literature. 2. Minerals in the body--Juvenile literature.   [1. Vitamins. 2. Minerals in nutrition. 3. Nutrition.]   I. Title. II. Series.
   QP771.R696 2003
   612.3'99--dc21
                                    2002012645

Acknowledgments
We would like to thank the following for permission to reproduce photographs: ©Corbis: pp. **31**, **32** (Paul Barton), **33** (Lester V. Bergman), **36**; ©Gareth Boden: pp. **16**, **19**, **20**, **23**, **27**, **30**; ©Getty Images: pp. **4** (PPG International/Bill Losh), **7** (FPG International/VCL), **40** (FPG International/Gibson); ©Liz Eddison: pp. **8**, **9**; ©Photodisc: p. **6**; ©Photolibrary Group Ltd: pp. **10** (Imagesource), **17** (Phototake Science/James CR. A.), **28** (Flirt Collection/Chris Rogers); ©SPL: pp. **14** (B. O. Veisland, MI&I), **15** (Eye of Science), **21** (Mark Clarke), **34** (Jim Varney), **35** (Biophoto Associates), **37** (John Paul Kay, Peter Arnold Inc.), **41** (Bettina Salomon); ©USDA Center for Nutrition Policy and Promotion p. **39**.

Cover photograph of green cabbage, reproduced with permission of ©PhotoLibrary Group/Photoalto/Isabelle Rozenbaum.

We would like to thank Dr. Sarah Schenker and Nicole A. Clark for their invaluable assistance in the preparation of this book.

Contents

Any words appearing in the text in bold, **like this**, are explained in the glossary.

Fueling the Body Machine

Your body works like a very complicated machine. Most machines involve electrical wiring, screws, and bolts, but the body uses chemicals and chemical processes instead. In fact, most of the body's functions rely on different **chemical reactions**. Your body makes some of these chemicals itself, but it has to take in all the rest from the outside world—**oxygen** from the air and a wide range of chemicals from food. The chemicals that come from food are called **nutrients**.

Nutrients

The main nutrients in food are **carbohydrates**, **fats**, and **proteins**. They supply your body with **energy** and the chemicals it needs to grow and replace **cells**. In addition to these main nutrients, your body needs small amounts of vitamins and minerals to help it carry out all the chemical processes that make it work. This book is about vitamins and minerals, but since most foods contain a mixture of different types of nutrients, we will take a look at the other nutrients first.

Carbohydrates

Foods rich in carbohydrate include **starchy** foods such as bread, potatoes, pasta, and rice, as well as sugary foods and drinks, such as cakes and candies. The body breaks down the starch and sugar in these foods to use for energy.

These basketball players are using up lots of energy as they dribble the ball, run, and jump. Most of their energy comes from eating foods that contain carbohydrates or fats.

Fats

Fats supply the body with energy, but in a more concentrated form than carbohydrates. If your body gets more energy than it needs, it stores the surplus (extra energy) as a layer of fat under your skin and around **organs**, such as your heart.

Protein

Your body is made of millions of tiny cells. Different types of cells make up your skin, muscles, and bones. Some cells do not last long before they have to be replaced. Cells consist mainly of water and protein, so to build new cells, your body uses proteins that you get from foods such as meat, fish, eggs, beans, and cheese. It is particularly important that children take in plenty of protein, because they are still growing and their bodies need it to make millions of extra cells.

This boy's height is being measured to see how tall he has grown. The protein in the cheese he is eating will help him to continue growing.

Small Quantities

Most food consists of water and the main nutrients—carbohydrates, fats, and proteins—but food also contains small amounts of vitamins and minerals. The fact that they only contain small amounts is fine, because your body only needs tiny amounts of each to stay healthy. The amounts are so small that most are measured as thousandth or hundredth parts of a gram. Nevertheless, without vitamins and minerals, you would soon become sick.

Too small to detect

Vitamins and minerals are needed in such small quantities that for centuries scientists did not know that most existed. They knew that to be healthy and to grow well, people needed to eat carbohydrates, fats, proteins, and some minerals. Since 1753 they had also known about the importance of fruit. Before then, sailors on long voyages often died of scurvy. Scurvy is a disease that stops wounds from healing well and causes blood to leak from the tiny blood vessels under the skin and in the gums. A ship's doctor named James Lind thought that the sailors' limited diet, which did not include fruits or vegetables, might be causing the scurvy. He tried adding various foods, but the scurvy only stopped when he gave the sailors lemons and oranges.

MINERALS IN THE BODY

About 1 percent of your body weight is calcium. This means that if you weigh 50 kilograms (110 pounds), you have about 500 grams (18 ounces) of calcium in your body. There is much less of other minerals in the body. Most adults, for example, have only about 3–4 grams (0.11–0.14 ounces) of iron in their bodies.

Lemons are a good source of vitamin C.

Discovery of vitamins

About 150 years later, in 1906, a scientist named Frederick Hopkins experimented with the diet of rats. He discovered that "astonishingly small amounts" of some substances are needed for the body to be able to use the main nutrients to grow and to thrive. Since then, scientists have come to understand in detail how the body uses both vitamins and minerals. Some are needed by all the cells in the body, while others, like the vitamin C in lemon juice, work in particular types of cells. Among other things, vitamin C is needed to build strong blood vessels and to help wounds heal. This book is about vitamins and minerals and what happens if you eat too much or too little of them.

Many foods contain small amounts of a few vitamins and minerals, so you need to eat a wide range of food, particularly vegetables and fruits, to get them all. The food in this shopping cart will keep a whole family well supplied with vitamins and minerals for a week.

What Are Vitamins?

Vitamins are chemical **compounds** that contain carbon and various other **elements** and are found in plants and animals. We know of 13 different vitamins that help our bodies carry out all the chemical processes needed to stay alive.

Identifying vitamins

Vitamins are sometimes known by their chemical names, but are often identified by a letter of the alphabet. For example, thiamin is often known as vitamin B_1 and ascorbic acid as vitamin C. Vitamins A, D, E, and K **dissolve** in fat and are carried into the body mainly in fatty or oily food. The rest, the B vitamins and vitamin C, dissolve in water.

Vitamin A

The chemical name of vitamin A is retinol. Retinol itself is only found in animal foods, particularly liver and cod liver oil. But many fruits and vegetables also contain carotenes (yellow or orange substances), which can be converted in the body to retinol and so count toward vitamin A. The most important carotene is beta-carotene, which is found in carrots, red peppers, sweet potatoes, spinach, and mangoes.

>>

Most vitamins are found in a range of food. These foods are good sources of vitamins A, D, E, or K, the vitamins that are **soluble** in fat.

B vitamins

Several different vitamins are included in a group
called the B vitamins. They are grouped together
because of the way the body uses them (see
pages 18–19), but many are also found in the
same foods. Milk, meat, green leafy vegetables such as
spinach, cereals, bread, and potatoes are good sources of several of
the B vitamins. Vitamin B_{12} is more difficult to get. It is found only in food
that comes from animals, such as meat, fish, eggs, cheese, and milk.

 Vitamin C and the B vitamins
are soluble in water. These
foods are rich in either the
B vitamins or vitamin C.
Some even have both.

Vitamin C

Vitamin C is found mainly in plants, including potatoes. In fact, the only
plants that do not contain vitamin C are cereals, dried peas, and beans. You
get much more vitamin C from eating fresh, raw fruits and vegetables than
from cooked ones, since it is easily destroyed when it is heated or stored.

Making vitamins in the body

Although vitamins D and K are found in various foods, your body can make
them itself. Vitamin D is sometimes called the "sunshine vitamin" because
when your skin is exposed to sunlight, the vitamin forms in your skin. You
take in some vitamin K from spinach, cabbage, cauliflower, peas, and cereal.
Vitamin K is also made inside your body by **bacteria** in the **large intestine**.

What Are Minerals?

Minerals are elements that are found in the ground. They include iron, zinc, and other metals that are used in industry. Living things need minerals, too, although only in small amounts. Living things cannot make minerals and so have to take them in from the outside world. Your body needs about 15 essential minerals to function and grow healthily. Some of these are particularly important and are called the major minerals. They are calcium, phosphorus, potassium, sodium, magnesium, iron, chloride, and zinc.

These nails are made mainly of iron. This metal is needed by your body to help it function properly.

How we get minerals

Small amounts of minerals are scattered throughout the soil, and some dissolve in water. Plants draw in water through their roots, with these minerals dissolved in it. The minerals are taken to all parts of the plant and are then passed on to any animals that eat them, so almost all our food contains some minerals. The foods that are richest in the major minerals are milk, meat, bread and other cereals, and vegetables.

Milk and meat

Milk and dairy products, such as cheese and yogurt, contain all the major minerals, although they are not a very good source of iron. Milk and cheese are especially rich in calcium, the mineral needed for strong bones and teeth. Meat, particularly liver, is the best source of iron, although other foods such as sardines, some fortified breakfast cereals, and chocolate also contain iron.

Bread, other cereals, and plants

Bread and other cereal-based food, such as pasta and rice, contain all the major minerals, although less potassium than other minerals. Bananas and other fruits and vegetables are good sources of potassium. Some vegetables are particularly rich in certain minerals. Watercress and okra, for example, contain calcium, while potatoes are rich in magnesium and potassium.

Salt

Table salt is made up of two elements, sodium and chlorine, combined together. Salt is naturally present in most foods, while some foods, such as bacon, chips, soy sauce, and cornflakes, have a lot of salt added to them. In addition, many people add salt to the food they eat, although their normal diet contains plenty of salt already.

TRACE ELEMENTS

In addition to the eight major minerals, your body needs tiny amounts of seven other minerals, including copper, chromium, fluoride, and iodine. We call these the **trace elements**. Apart from fluoride, these minerals are available in common foods. Fluoride makes teeth stronger and is added to most toothpastes and to some sources of tap water.

Digesting Vitamins and Minerals

Food contains the vitamins and minerals you need, but it has to be digested before your body can use them. The process of digestion breaks up food into smaller and smaller pieces. Digestion begins in your mouth and continues in your stomach and **small intestine**. Special chemicals called **enzymes** help to break down carbohydrates, fats, and proteins into separate **molecules** and parts of molecules. Vitamins and minerals do not need to be broken down, but are taken into the blood with water or fats.

In the mouth

As you chew food, your teeth mash it up and mix it with **saliva** until it forms a soft, mushy lump. Then your tongue pushes it to the back of your mouth and you swallow it. It passes down your throat, through your **pharynx** into your **esophagus**, and into your stomach.

In the stomach

Your stomach is like a blender. As it churns the food around and mixes it with digestive juice made in the wall of the stomach, the food slowly turns into a type of thick soup called **chyme**. The valve at the bottom of the stomach opens from time to time and a squirt of chyme passes to the small intestine, where the next stage occurs.

In the duodenum

The first part of the small intestine is called the **duodenum**. In adults, the duodenum is 23–28 centimeters (9–11 inches) long, and it is supplied with **bile** from the gall bladder and digestive juices from the walls of the small intestine and from the pancreas.

Bile is made in the liver and stored in the gall bladder. It acts on fats in the same way that liquid dish detergent does—bile breaks fats up into tiny globules or droplets so that they can be digested.

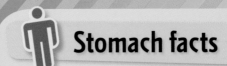

Stomach facts

Your stomach stretches as it fills up with food. How long the food stays in the stomach depends on what it is and how much there is of it, but on average food stays in your stomach for about two to three hours.

The rest of the small intestine

As the chyme passes through the small intestine, it is swirled back and forth. This helps the digestive juices to mix with the chyme and get to work. Digestive juices contain enzymes, which are chemicals that the body makes to break fats, carbohydrates, and proteins into smaller units. Fats take the longest to break up. It is not until they reach the end of the small intestine that most are absorbed into the blood.

The digestive system

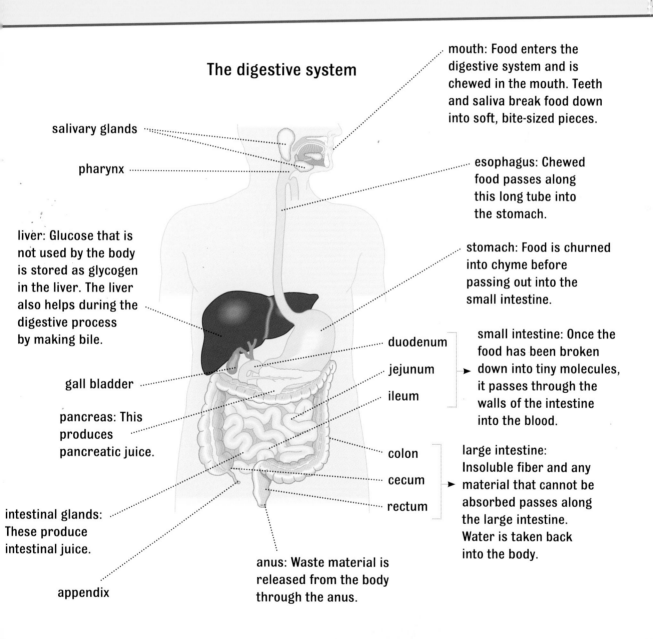

salivary glands

pharynx

liver: Glucose that is not used by the body is stored as glycogen in the liver. The liver also helps during the digestive process by making bile.

gall bladder

pancreas: This produces pancreatic juice.

intestinal glands: These produce intestinal juice.

appendix

mouth: Food enters the digestive system and is chewed in the mouth. Teeth and saliva break food down into soft, bite-sized pieces.

esophagus: Chewed food passes along this long tube into the stomach.

stomach: Food is churned into chyme before passing out into the small intestine.

duodenum

jejunum

ileum

small intestine: Once the food has been broken down into tiny molecules, it passes through the walls of the intestine into the blood.

colon

cecum

rectum

large intestine: Insoluble fiber and any material that cannot be absorbed passes along the large intestine. Water is taken back into the body.

anus: Waste material is released from the body through the anus.

Absorbing Vitamins and Minerals

When carbohydrates, fats, and proteins have been broken down into small enough pieces, they are ready to be absorbed into the blood. Most nutrients, including minerals and vitamins, are absorbed through the walls of the stomach and small intestine. Some pass through the liver, which processes and returns them to the blood for the rest of the body to use.

The villi

The walls of the small intestine are covered in tiny finger-like bumps called villi. Although the villi are extremely small, each one no more than half a millimeter (0.02 inch) long, they increase the surface area of the intestine wall considerably. This means the digested food has a greater chance of being absorbed. The walls of the villi are so thin that molecules of digested food pass through them and are absorbed into the tiny blood vessels inside.

Absorbing water

As food is broken down, the water in it is squeezed out. Water passes easily through the walls of the villi into the blood and carries with it whatever is dissolved in it. Minerals, vitamin C, and some of the B vitamins are absorbed in the duodenum, the first part of the small intestine. More B vitamins are absorbed in the rest of the small intestine.

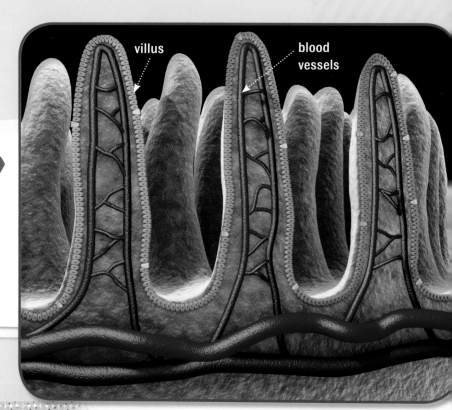

villus

blood vessels

The small intestine is lined with villi. Molecules of digested food pass through the walls of the villus and the blood vessels into the blood.

Absorbing fat-soluble vitamins

Bile breaks up fats into tiny droplets, which are then digested by enzymes. They break the large fat molecules into smaller units called **fatty acids**. As the fatty acids are absorbed into the blood, the vitamins dissolved in them are also absorbed.

Not all vitamins and minerals are absorbed

Some vitamins and minerals are dependent on other factors being present for their absorption. For example, vitamin C helps iron and calcium to be absorbed. Some foods, such as tea, coffee, and wheat, contain substances that make it less likely that iron or other nutrients are absorbed.

The large intestine

Anything that is not absorbed in the small intestine passes through to the large intestine. Here, millions of bacteria help to process the waste material. While this is happening, the bacteria manufacture vitamin K, which passes into the blood. At the same time, water passes from the undigested mush into the blood; the waste food, mixed with digestive juices, bacteria, and other waste matter, slowly becomes more solid. This solid waste is pushed out of the body through the anus.

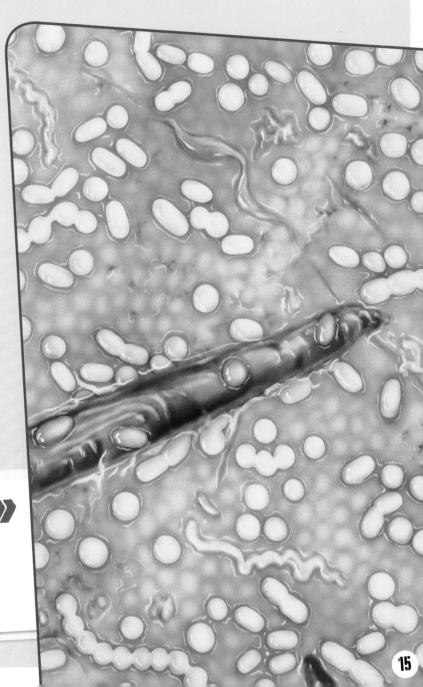

Bacteria in the large intestine manufacture vitamin K. The bacteria mix with the feces, giving it its foul smell.

How the Body Uses Vitamins

Vitamins are needed by all the millions of cells in the body and are essential for them to work properly. Most vitamins perform several different functions. Most do some work in all cells, but some vitamins work in particular types of cells. For example, folate, one of the B vitamins, is used in the **bone marrow** to produce new red blood cells.

Helping cells

Vitamins form part of many enzymes. This means that they are needed for a **chemical change** to take place, but they are not part of the reaction. The main nutrients in food, for example, give your body energy and the materials to build new cells. However, your body cannot use the main nutrients without the help of vitamins and minerals. They allow the cells to change fats and the sugar from carbohydrates into energy. Others help the cells to use proteins to build new cells and repair existing cells.

This girl is making herself a snack that is rich in carbohydrates, but her body cannot turn the carbohydrates into energy without the help of vitamins.

Defending against cancer

Some vitamins help to prevent **free radical** damage, which can lead to cancer. As the body carries out its normal chemical reactions, it produces chemicals called free radicals. Free radicals can damage protein and **DNA** in the body's cells. DNA is the molecule that contains your **genetic code** and tells your body how to build and repair itself. If the cells cannot repair the damage, they may become cancer cells. Vitamins C and E, selenium, sulfur, and some beta-carotenes combat these dangerous free radicals. They are known as **antioxidants**.

Preventing heart disease

A good intake of fruits and vegetables may be protective against certain diseases such as heart disease. Consuming a diet high in saturates can increase levels of LDL **cholesterol** (bad cholesterol) in the blood. It can accumulate in the vessel walls of the heart and become oxidized (damaged), causing the vessels to become clogged and narrow. Fruits and vegetables contain important vitamins and minerals and other substances, which act as antioxidants. Antioxidants prevent cells of the heart and surrounding vessels from being damaged by free radicals.

Vitamin A

Vitamin A makes your skin, hair, and nails healthy, but it does not work if you rub it into your hair or skin. Vitamins only work from inside the body. Vitamin A also helps children to grow well. This is because the body needs vitamin A to produce new cells.

SEEING IN THE DARK

Carrots really do help you to see in the dark. They do not give you night vision, but they are rich in vitamin A. The cells in your eyes need vitamin A to help them detect dim light. Without it, you would be blind at night.

This is a close-up picture of an eye showing the optic nerve. You can keep your eyes healthy by eating plenty of foods containing vitamin A.

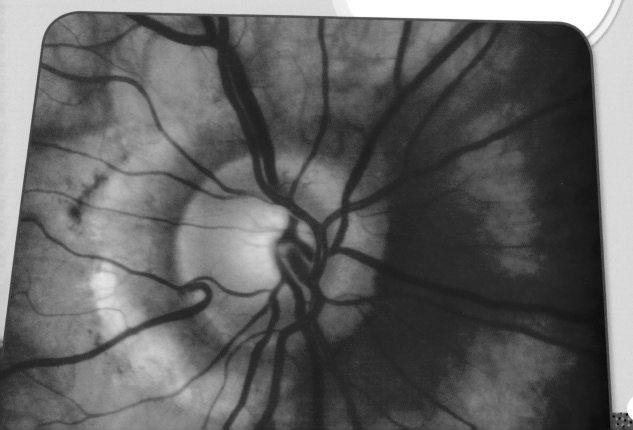

Using B Vitamins and Vitamin C

Both B vitamins and vitamin C are soluble in water. You need a constant supply of them, because your body cannot store them. Some B vitamins help your cells change food into energy, while others build up new proteins. Vitamin C helps to keep your skin, bones, and other **tissues** healthy.

Releasing energy from food

The B vitamins thiamin, riboflavin, and niacin are all needed by the cells to release energy from food. Thiamin works on carbohydrates, while riboflavin helps to release the energy in fats and proteins as well as carbohydrates. Two more B vitamins—pantothenic acid and biotin—are essential for your body to use the energy in fats.

Using protein

During digestion, protein in your food is broken down into units called **amino acids**. Vitamin B_6 helps your cells rebuild the amino acids into new proteins. One of these proteins is **hemoglobin**, the substance that makes red blood cells red. Hemoglobin takes in oxygen from the air you breathe in and carries it to the rest of the body. Vitamin B_6 can also manufacture the B vitamin niacin from one of the amino acids.

Vitamin B_{12} and folate

Vitamin B_{12} and folate are needed in parts of the body where cells are being made very quickly. For example, your bone marrow—the soft jelly in the middle of some bones—manufactures about 100 million new red blood cells every minute. It cannot manage this without vitamin B_{12} and folate. Both of these vitamins also help to form healthy nerve cells.

COOK YOUR EGGS

Egg yolks contain the B vitamin biotin, but your body can only use it if the egg is cooked. Otherwise a substance contained in raw egg white combines with biotin and prevents the body from using it.

Connective tissue

Vitamin C is needed to produce collagen, the substance that forms the structure of your skin, bones, teeth, and connective tissue. Connective tissue is strong but stretchy. It keeps your heart, lungs, stomach, and other organs in place, but allows them to move as you bend, twist, and stretch. Other examples of connective tissue include gums, which hold your teeth in your jaws; tendons, which attach your muscles to your bones; and ligaments, which hold your joints together.

Other uses of vitamin C

Vitamin C builds strong blood vessels and helps wounds to heal. Vitamin C also helps with the absorption of iron from foods other than meat.

Kiwi, oranges, grapefruit, and black currants are just some of the fruits that are particularly rich in vitamin C. Eating them will help to keep this girl's gums, teeth, and other tissues healthy.

Using Vitamins D, E, and K

Vitamins D, E, and K, like vitamin A, are all soluble in fat. This means that the body can store them. Each one has a particular function in the body.

Vitamin D

The main task of vitamin D is to help your body absorb the mineral calcium. Much of the vitamin D in your body is made by sunlight acting on your skin, but if you usually keep your skin covered, you need to take in the vitamin from food. The liver and the kidneys process vitamin D. They turn it into a substance that controls the amount of calcium that is absorbed into the blood through your digestive system.

Calcium in the bones

Calcium also needs vitamin D after it has been absorbed into the blood. Most of the calcium you eat is deposited in your bones and teeth, where it makes them strong and rigid. However, scientists think that without vitamin D, your bones and teeth cannot take the calcium in.

This girl is getting vitamin D from two sources: the yogurt and sunlight. Vitamin D will help the calcium in the yogurt form strong bones and teeth.

Vitamin E

Vitamin E is most important in the body as an antioxidant. This means that it helps to prevent damage by the chemicals called free radicals, which can cause cancer and heart disease. At the same time, vitamin E has several other functions, including its structural role in cells. It is also needed by the **immune system**.

Vitamin K

Vitamin K helps blood to clot and wounds to heal. If you cut yourself, blood flows from the tiny blood vessels in your skin. Several chemicals make the blood in the wound become thicker and form a clot. The clot plugs the wound and hardens to form a scab, which protects the wound while the blood vessels heal and new skin grows.

Blood facts

Blood can carry the bacteria and **viruses** that cause serious diseases. If you help someone with a cut, don't let his or her blood touch your skin or get inside your body. Always cover cuts with a clean bandage.

A cut or graze should not bleed for long. Soon the blood clots and blocks the wound. Vitamin K helps the blood to clot and the wound to heal.

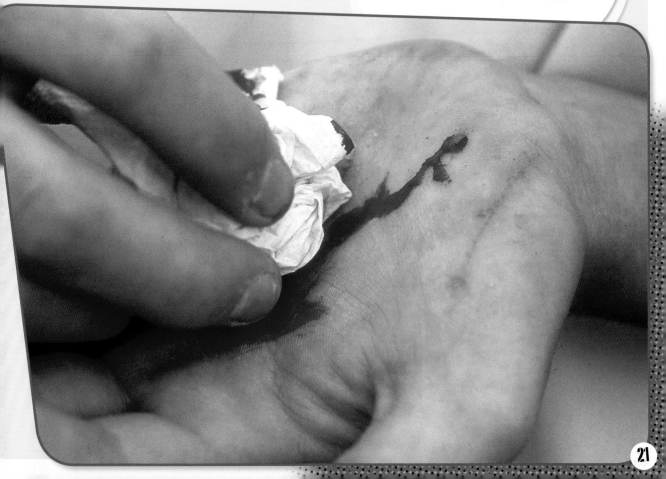

21

How the Body Uses Minerals

Minerals are used throughout the body, both inside and outside the cells. They have three main functions. Some make your bones and teeth strong and rigid. Others become part of your cells and body fluids, such as blood and sweat. The rest are needed to make enzymes, the substances that help your cells carry out chemical reactions.

Bones

The minerals that make bones and teeth hard are calcium, phosphorus, and magnesium. Your bones use 99 percent of the calcium, 75 percent of the phosphorus, and half of the magnesium in your body. Without them, your bones would still be strong, but they would be flexible like cartilage, the substance that you can feel at the tips of your ears.

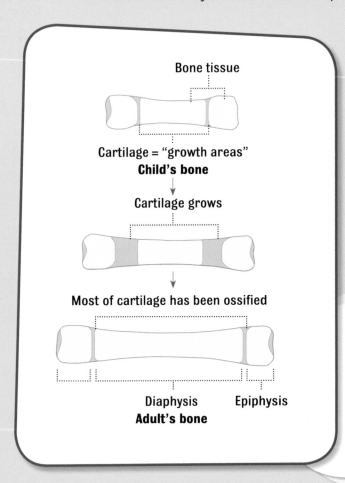

Bone tissue

Cartilage = "growth areas"
Child's bone

↓

Cartilage grows

↓

Most of cartilage has been ossified

Diaphysis   Epiphysis
Adult's bone

Calcium store

Calcium can move in and out of your bones if it is needed elsewhere. Muscles work by contracting (getting shorter), but they need calcium to be able to do this. Your heart is a muscle, and it also needs calcium. Bones act as a store of calcium in case your body is not taking in enough from food.

 A child's bone contains much more cartilage than an adult's bone. As the cartilage absorbs minerals and changes into bone (ossifies), the child's bone slowly grows, and new cartilage forms at the ends.

Absorbing calcium

Your body takes in less than half the amount of calcium your food contains. Several factors can reduce this amount even further. You need vitamin D in order to absorb calcium and deposit it in your bones, so if you are lacking in vitamin D you will take in less calcium. Some foods, particularly spinach and rhubarb, contain chemicals that stop calcium from being absorbed into the blood. This does not mean that you should never eat spinach and rhubarb, but that you should eat calcium-rich food separately.

Fluoride

Fluoride is a trace element (see page 11) that makes your teeth less likely to decay. Bacteria in your mouth feed on sugar and produce a strong acid that dissolves enamel, the hard coating on your teeth. Once the acid has made a hole in the enamel of a tooth, it can eat its way through the **dentin** below, causing your tooth to rot. Fluoride works best on your teeth while they are still forming. Your baby teeth form before you are born, but your adult teeth are slowly forming until you are about 10 years old.

DISSOLVING BONE

If you put a chicken bone in a container with vinegar and leave it, the minerals in the bone will slowly dissolve. After a few weeks the bone will have become flexible, like the cartilage it formed from.

Using toothpaste that contains flouride helps to prevent your teeth from decaying.

Minerals in Body Fluids

Your body is awash with liquid. Apart from blood, sweat, tears, and other body fluids, every cell contains liquid. These fluids are mainly water with minerals and other substances dissolved in them. Minerals in the water inside and outside your cells control what passes into and out of the cells. Salt, containing the elements sodium and chlorine, helps to control the amount of water in your body.

Salt in the body

All your body fluids, including blood, urine, tears, mucus, and sweat, contain salt. The amounts of salt and other minerals in your body are controlled by your kidneys. They make sure that the concentration of salt in your blood stays about the same. If your blood contains extra salt, you will feel thirsty and drink extra water. If your blood is low in salt, your kidneys get rid of extra water to keep the concentration of salt about the same.

Sweat

If you lick your skin when you have been sweating, it will taste salty. Sweating helps to control the temperature of the body. At the same time, your body loses water and minerals, particularly salt. If the weather is very hot, or if you have been sweating due to exercise, you should take in extra water and salt to make up for what is lost.

Border crossing

Blood carries the nutrients from digested food to every cell in your body. Each cell is surrounded by salty water. The liquid inside each cell, however, contains potassium, magnesium, and phosphorus. The difference between these liquids allows nutrients and oxygen to pass from the blood into the cell. It also allows waste chemicals, such as proteins and **carbon dioxide**, to pass from the cell into the blood. The blood carries the waste away to be expelled from the body.

CHLOE'S STORY

Chloe was feeling very angry and tired. There had been particularly hot weather for several weeks, and she kept getting cramps in her legs. She knew she should drink extra water in hot weather, but she didn't realize that sweating had left her body short of salt. Then one night she and a friend shared a huge package of salty crackers. Chloe was amazed to find she no longer felt tired, and the cramps went away, too.

Water fact

About two-thirds of your body is water. In an adult this includes about 4.5 liters (9.5 pints) of blood, 3 liters (6.3 pints) of digestive juices, and about 250 milliliters (0.5 pints) of urine. The rest is liquid in and around the cells and internal tubes.

Your body takes in and loses water every day. Salt in the body helps to keep a balance between the water you take in and the water lost.

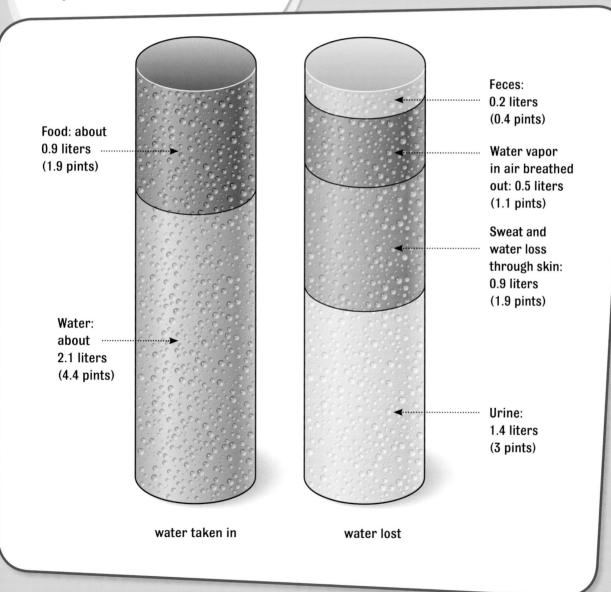

Food: about 0.9 liters (1.9 pints)

Water: about 2.1 liters (4.4 pints)

Feces: 0.2 liters (0.4 pints)

Water vapor in air breathed out: 0.5 liters (1.1 pints)

Sweat and water loss through skin: 0.9 liters (1.9 pints)

Urine: 1.4 liters (3 pints)

water taken in

water lost

Minerals in Enzymes

Minerals and some vitamins form part of many enzymes. We have already seen how enzymes work in the digestive system (see page 12), but enzymes also act inside every single body cell. A single cell may have hundreds of reactions going on at the same time, each using a different enzyme. Enzymes speed up the rate at which chemicals react, and cells would not be able to survive without them.

Taking in oxygen

More than half the iron in your body is in your blood. It is contained in hemoglobin, the red substance in red blood cells. As blood passes through the lungs, oxygen from the air you breathe in becomes attached to hemoglobin. Later, as the blood is pumped around the body, the oxygen leaves the hemoglobin and passes into the cells.

Losing carbon dioxide

Oxygen combines with sugar to produce energy inside the cell. As it does so, carbon dioxide is produced. This gas passes out of the cell and attaches itself to hemoglobin that has lost its oxygen. The carbon dioxide leaves the blood in the lungs and is breathed out.

All the living cells in your body need to take in oxygen and get rid of waste carbon dioxide. Red blood cells, which contain iron, transport oxygen from the lungs to the cells and return waste carbon dioxide to the lungs.

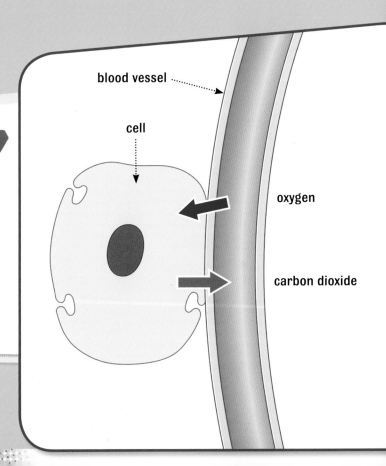

blood vessel

cell

oxygen

carbon dioxide

Iron in the body

What happens to the rest of the iron in your body? Some of it is used by the muscles, and the rest is stored in your liver. Other animals store iron in their liver, too, which makes eating liver a good source of this mineral. When red blood cells die, the iron in the hemoglobin is reused, so your body loses iron only when you lose blood. Iron is not easily absorbed into the body and needs vitamin C for even a quarter of the iron in food to pass into the blood.

Zinc

Zinc, like iron, is a major mineral (see page 10). It works with many different enzymes. It is needed for children to grow and for their bodies to become sexually mature at **puberty**. In addition, zinc helps wounds to heal.

Trace elements

Most of the minerals known as trace elements (fluoride, copper, selenium, manganese, chromium, and cobalt) are used mainly by different enzymes. Iodine forms a part of the **hormones** produced by the **thyroid gland**. These hormones control your **metabolic rate**.

This girl is using a special cream to soothe her **eczema**. The cream contains zinc, which will help to make the skin less inflamed.

Too Much of a Good Thing

Your body needs so little of each vitamin and mineral that swallowing vitamin and mineral pills can easily give your body much more than it needs. Too much of some vitamins and minerals can harm you.

Supplements

Many supplements are sold as cures for various conditions, or simply to make you extra healthy. Normally, if you eat a wide variety of foods, you will get plenty of each type of vitamin and mineral. In some cases, however, supplements can be useful (see pages 40 and 41).

 These are just some of the many vitamin and mineral supplements that are sold. You should check with your doctor before taking supplements, however, because excessive amounts of some vitamins and minerals can be harmful. If you eat a varied and healthy diet, you should not need supplements.

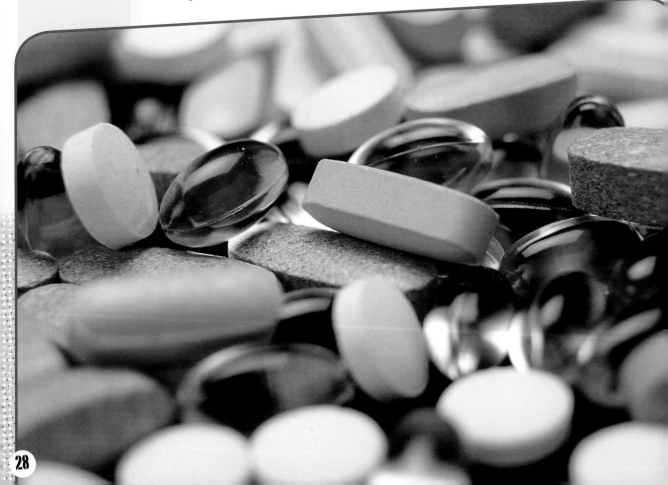

Water-soluble vitamins

It does not matter if you have too much of vitamin C or most B vitamins. They are soluble in water, and any extra is just filtered by your kidneys into your urine. There are a few exceptions to this, however. If you take too much niacin, one of the B vitamins, it can make your face and hands feel as if they are burning and it can damage your liver. Too much vitamin B_6 can harm your sensory nerves—the nerves that carry signals to your brain from your senses.

> ## CAN VITAMIN C CURE COLDS?
>
> Some people take up to 250 times the recommended amount of vitamin C, claiming that it can cure the common cold. Most scientists disagree and say that there is no evidence to support such a claim.

Fat-soluble vitamins

If you take in more fat-soluble vitamins than your body needs, your liver stores the excess. This means that if your diet is short of vitamins A, D, E, or K for a short time, your body will simply draw on supplies from the liver. It is now thought that too much vitamin E can cause heart problems and cause problems with the absorption of vitamin K. Too much of vitamins A and D can also harm you.

Too much vitamin A

If you take in too much vitamin A, the extra can poison your liver. Unborn babies are most at risk from being damaged by too much vitamin A. Pregnant women should avoid eating liver, or things made of liver, such as liverwurst or pâté, because the excessive amounts of vitamin A in liver can cause **birth defects** in their babies.

Too much vitamin D

Vitamin D controls how much calcium is absorbed into the body, so too much vitamin D can lead to an excess of calcium. Extra calcium is usually filtered out in your urine, but if there is more than your kidneys can cope with, the extra can damage them. Young children, in particular, should not have too much vitamin D in their diets.

Too Much Salt and Other Minerals

If you eat a balanced diet you will get enough—but not too much—of most minerals. However, many people eat more salt than they need, and this gives some people health problems. Babies are particularly at risk from too much salt or phosphorus, while too much fluoride can discolor your teeth.

Added salt

There is enough natural salt in food to supply people's needs, but salt makes food tastier and it is usually added when food is cooked. In addition, we often sprinkle salt onto the food on our plates. Scientists calculate that, on average, most people eat twice the amount of salt they need, and some eat even more.

High blood pressure

If your blood contains extra salt, your kidneys filter out much of it. But the kidneys also keep extra water in the blood to balance the excess salt. This increases the volume of blood in your body and can cause high blood pressure. Blood pressure measures the force with which the heart pumps blood into the **arteries**. High blood pressure can damage the heart, cause **strokes**, and damage the kidneys.

Chips, peanuts, other salty snacks, bacon, and many TV dinners are very high in salt. You should keep your intake of these food products to a minimum.

Babies

A baby's kidneys cannot get rid of extra salt, which then damages their kidneys. Extra salt should never be added to a baby's or a toddler's food. There is enough natural salt in food to supply them with all the sodium and chlorine they need. Newborn babies must be fed on breast milk or special formula milk, because ordinary cows' milk contains too much phosphorus for them.

Too much fluoride

Extra fluoride makes your teeth strong and less likely to need fillings, but some children receive more fluoride than they need. Most brands of toothpaste contain fluoride, and, in some places, fluoride is added to the tap water. You should not take fluoride pills if fluoride is already added to the drinking water. Extra fluoride will make your teeth extra strong, but it may discolor them.

MERCURY IN FISH

Large fish, particularly swordfish, shark, and marlin, have high levels of mercury in their flesh. The mercury is washed off the land into the sea. Mercury damages the **nervous system**, so children under 16 years old and pregnant women should not eat these fish.

Fluoride is added to some drinking water. Too much of it can discolor your teeth.

Deficiency Diseases

Eating a balanced and varied diet gives your body all the vitamins and minerals you need. However, people who do not get enough of just one of these essential nutrients can suffer from a range of problems. A shortage of a particular vitamin or mineral can cause one of many deficiency diseases.

Who suffers from deficiency diseases?

Some people have a medical condition that makes it hard for them to absorb a particular vitamin or mineral. Other people eat such a limited diet that they deprive their bodies of essential nutrients. However, the people who are most likely to suffer from deficiency diseases are the millions of people throughout the world who are starving or who cannot afford to eat a good diet. Even in rich countries, there are many people, particularly elderly people or very poor people, who cannot afford to feed themselves properly.

Effects of deficiency diseases

Vitamins and minerals each perform many different functions in the body. This means that a deficiency disease usually affects the body in a number of ways, making a sufferer feel sick and weak. The person's skin, muscles, blood, or bones may be particularly affected.

Old people are more at risk of developing some deficiency diseases than younger people. As people get older, more effort needs to be made to stay fit and healthy.

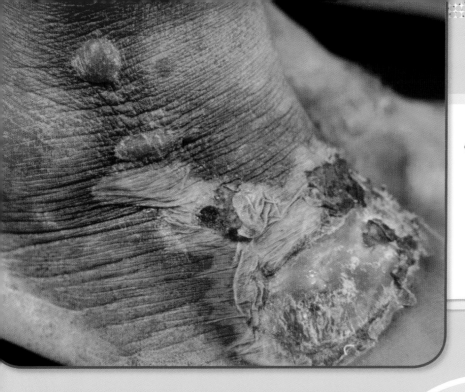

This person is suffering from pellagra, caused by a lack of niacin. The skin around the ankle has become sore and irritated.

Pellagra

Pellagra is caused by a lack of niacin and other B vitamins. It is common among people who eat mainly corn, since it does not contain much niacin. People feel weak, but not hungry, and they suffer from indigestion and **diarrhea**. Their skin becomes irritated, dark, and scaly, particularly where it is exposed to sunlight.

Beriberi

Beriberi is caused by a lack of the B vitamin thiamin in the diet. It used to be common in China, Japan, and Southeast Asia, where people ate "polished" rice, which is rice that contains no thiamin. The name of the disease means "I cannot" and describes how sufferers become too sick to do anything. Their legs become stiff, paralyzed, and painful. Today, artificial thiamin is added to white rice, and the disease has become less common.

BODY STORES

Your body stores some minerals and vitamins, particularly the vitamins that are soluble in fats. Your liver, for example, can store enough vitamin D to last you for two years.

Other Vitamin Deficiencies

Not enough vitamin A

A deficiency of vitamin A affects the nerve endings in the eyes that detect dim light. This makes it hard to see in the dark and can lead to a person being blind at night. A lack of vitamin A also makes it harder for your body to fight off **infectious** diseases and can make you grow more slowly.

Not enough B vitamins

Your body cannot store B vitamins, so a shortage of them can affect your health after just a few months. Apart from beriberi and pellagra (see page 33), a shortage of vitamin B_{12} or of folate can cause **anemia**. Anemia means that people do not have enough healthy red blood cells to keep their cells supplied with oxygen. It makes them feel tired and lack energy.

Not enough vitamin C

A shortage of vitamin C can cause a lack of iron (see page 37). In extreme cases, lack of vitamin C stops the body from being able to heal. This condition is called scurvy. The small blood vessels that supply your cells become weak, and blood spills out under the skin. It is particularly noticeable in the gums and mouth, which both become sore. People's gums bleed and their teeth become loose.

Scientists use microscopes to check whether a sample of blood is anemic. They count the number of healthy red blood cells in the sample.

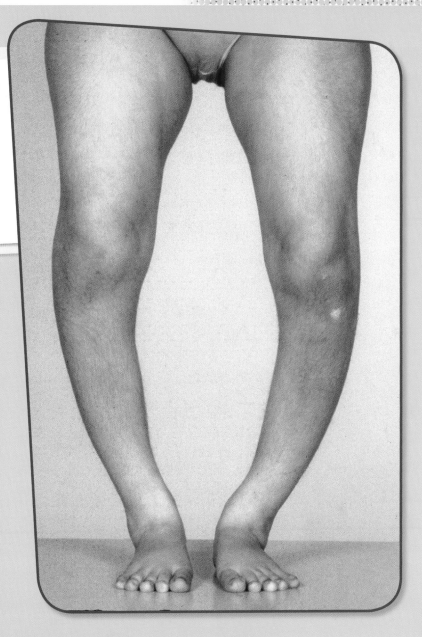

Rickets is a disease that can make you bowlegged. It is caused by eating food that lacks vitamin D or calcium when you are young.

Not enough vitamin D

Since vitamin D controls how much calcium your body absorbs and uses, a lack of vitamin D leads to a lack of calcium. Children need plenty of vitamin D and calcium because their bones are still growing. If they do not get enough, they may develop rickets. This means that their bones do not grow strong and straight.

Not enough vitamin E

Your body stores vitamin E in the fat that lies under your skin. It is unlikely that your diet will lack vitamin E. The only people who are at risk are people whose bodies cannot absorb the vitamin and **premature** babies. Babies that are born early have very little body fat and so have very little stored vitamin E. Unless they are given extra vitamin E, they become anemic.

Not enough vitamin K

A shortage of vitamin K will cause blood not to clot properly. This means that if you cut yourself, the wound will bleed much more and for far longer than it should. This deficiency is very unlikely to happen, however, because your body constantly makes vitamin K in your large intestine. A small number of newborn babies are short of the vitamin, so babies are usually given extra vitamin K as soon as they are born.

Mineral Deficiencies

Not enough calcium

Children and young adults need to eat plenty of foods that contain calcium. Children who do not get enough calcium may develop rickets. Even after a person has stopped growing, calcium is still added to the bones until peak bone mass is reached. People who do not reach their peak bone mass when they are younger are at risk of developing osteoporosis when they are older. This is a condition that makes bones break easily.

Not enough salt

If you often get muscle cramps, you may be suffering from lack of salt, particularly if the weather is hot or you often take part in sports that make you sweat. When you sweat, your body loses salt as well as water. Drinking plenty of water during exercise will help. Lack of salt can make you feel tired and sick.

Runners drink sports drinks that contain salt as well as water. This replaces the salt they lose through sweating.

Not enough potassium or magnesium

The people most likely to be deficient in potassium or magnesium are those who are suffering from a disease called kwashiorkor, caused by a lack of protein. Diseases that cause severe and long-lasting diarrhea may also lead to a shortage of potassium or magnesium. If this happens, the person may have a heart attack and die.

Not enough iron

A shortage of iron is one of the most common causes of anemia. Lack of iron means that the body cannot produce hemoglobin, and this leads to a shortage of red blood cells. Not having enough red blood cells stops cells in your body from getting all the oxygen they need.

Not enough iodine

People who do not get enough iodine in their diet suffer from a disease of the thyroid gland known as goiter. The gland swells up, and the neck can become huge.

DAVID'S GRANDMOTHER'S STORY

David's grandmother broke her leg and her arm when she tripped over a rug in her home. The fall was not bad, but, like many elderly women, she suffers from osteoporosis. Her bones have lost a lot of calcium and have become very brittle. Once the calcium has been lost, old people cannot replace it. David's mother is determined that she will not suffer from osteoporosis when she is older. She is planning to keep exercising and to eat foods that contain plenty of calcium.

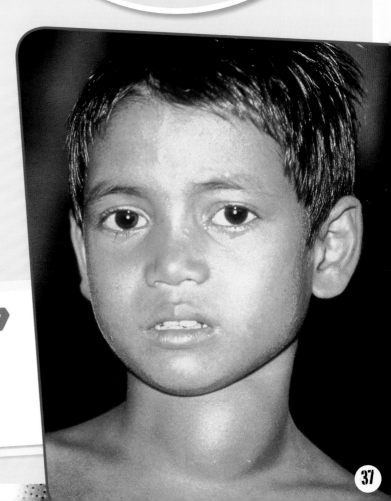

The swelling on this boy's neck is a result of an enlarged thyroid gland. He is suffering from goiter, a condition caused by a lack of iodine.

Healthy Eating

As long as you eat a varied diet, you should get all the vitamins and minerals you need. Any type of food contains only small amounts of some vitamins and minerals, so you need to eat many different types of food to make sure that you get all of them. The "MyPyramid" food pyramid divides foods into five groups (plus oils) and shows the types and proportions of foods that make a healthy diet.

1 – Grains

The grains group includes rice, pasta, breakfast cereals, bread, and potatoes. These foods all contain a lot of carbohydrates and will keep your body supplied with energy. They also contain many vitamins and minerals. Eat about 140 grams (5 ounces) from this group a day.

2 – Vegetables

Vegetables are rich in vitamins and minerals and in **fiber**. Fiber is the part of the food that your body cannot digest, so you might think it is unimportant. However, fiber is essential for your digestive system to work efficiently. Eat at least 2 cups of vegetables a day.

3 – Fruits

Fruits are also rich in vitamins, minerals, and fiber. Eat at least 1.5 cups of fruits a day.

4 – Milk

The milk group includes milk as well as cheese and yogurt. These foods provide proteins, fats, fat-soluble vitamins (A, D, E, and K), and many minerals, particularly calcium. Eat or drink about 3 cups a day from this group.

5 – Meat and beans

Foods in this group include meat, poultry, fish, eggs, nuts, and pulses (beans, peas, and lentils). This group is rich in proteins, which your body needs to repair and build new cells. Meat, fish, and eggs come from animals and are particularly rich in B vitamins and iron. Eat about 120 to 150 grams (4 to 5 ounces) a day.

The "MyPyramid" shows the wide variety of food you should eat to enjoy a balanced diet. It is divided into five main groups of food, plus oils.

RULES FOR HEALTHY EATING

- Eat a wide variety of food.
- Eat most food from groups 1, 2, and 3.
- Eat only a little food with a lot of fat, oil, or sugar.

| GRAINS | VEGETABLES | FRUITS | MILK | MEAT & BEANS |

Special Requirements

While most people can get all the vitamins and minerals they need by eating a varied and balanced diet, some groups of people need to take extra vitamins or minerals. They can do this by choosing foods that are rich in the nutrients they need, or by taking supplements in the form of vitamin and mineral pills.

Vegans

Vegetarian diets include dairy foods and contain all the vitamins and minerals people need, but vegans do not eat any food that comes from animals. They have to plan their diet carefully to make sure that it does not lack vitamin B$_{12}$. They can take this important vitamin in the form of a vitamin pill.

Pregnant women

When a woman is pregnant, her body diverts resources to the baby growing inside her, so she has to make sure she takes in enough for herself, too. In particular, she needs extra iron, calcium, and vitamins C and D so the baby can build strong bones and red blood cells. Pregnant women are usually given extra folate, or folic acid, to protect their unborn babies from a condition called **spina bifida**. Pregnant women should avoid liver because it is very rich in vitamin A, and too much vitamin A can cause birth defects. They should also avoid certain fish (see page 31).

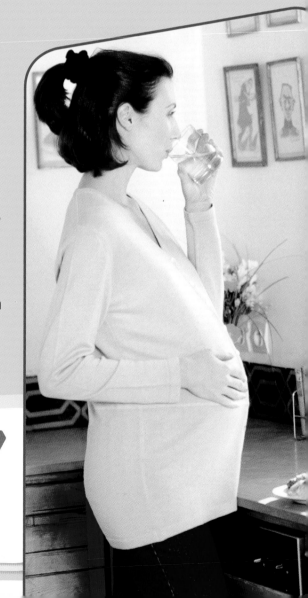

During pregnancy, women must eat food that contains plenty of vitamins and minerals and avoid eating liver and certain fish.

Babies and young children

Babies get all the nutrients they need from their mother's breast milk. Once breast-feeding has stopped, however, it is important that they receive a nourishing diet that includes all the vitamins they need, but not extra salt (see page 31). Many babies and young children are given drops that contain extra vitamins A, C, and D.

Older people

As people grow older, they tend to eat less. They have to be extra careful to make sure they are receiving sufficient amounts of all nutrients, including vitamins and minerals. Elderly people who cannot go outside are not able to make vitamin D from sunlight. They may lack this vitamin, so they should eat foods providing vitamin D.

Athletes

Athletes are usually very careful about the food they eat and make sure their bodies are fit and healthy. However, if they take part in endurance events or sports that make them sweat a lot for many hours, they have to drink extra liquid during the event.

This baby is learning to feed himself. Parents must make sure that the food their children eat is healthy. Many baby foods have vitamins and minerals specially added to them.

Nutritional Information

The two tables on this page show how much of some vitamins and minerals you should have every day. Some food labels tell you how much sodium the food contains. Salt is sodium chloride, so the figure for sodium tells you how much salt is in the food. It is recommended that adults should have no more than 2,300 milligrams (0.08 ounces) of sodium per day, which is about 6 grams (0.2 ounces) of salt.

Recommended daily intake of some vitamins

A µg (microgram) is one millionth of a gram.
An mg (milligram) is one thousandth of a gram.

Age	A (µg)	B₁ (mg)	B₁₂ (µg)	Folate (µg)	C (mg)
7–10	500	0.7	1.0	150	30
11–14 (girls)	600	0.7	1.2	200	35
11–14 (boys)	600	0.9	1.2	200	35

Recommended daily amounts of some minerals

Age	Calcium (mg)	Iron (mg)	Zinc (mg)	Sodium (mg)
7–10	550	8.7	7.0	2,000
11–19 (girls)	800	14.8	9.0	2,400
11–19 (boys)	1,000	11.3	9.5	2,400

EXTRA VITAMIN C

When your body is under **stress**, it uses up vitamin C faster. Smoking puts your body under constant stress. The best thing to do for your body and your health is to not smoke!

This table shows how many milligrams (mg) of some vitamins and minerals are contained in 100 grams (3.5 ounces) of different foods. (A thousand milligrams make a gram.)

Food (100-gram portion)	Thiamin (mg)	Vitamin C (mg)	Calcium (mg)	Iron (mg)	Sodium (mg)
Spaghetti (boiled and unsalted)	0.01	0	7	0.50	0
Boiled white rice	0.01	0	10	0.20	1
White bread	0.21	0	110	1.60	3
Cornflakes	2.1	22	4	29	723
Baked potatoes	0.37	14	11	0.70	12
Raw cabbage	0.1	3	40	0.5	18
Cucumber	0.03	2	18	0.30	3
Boiled spinach	0.1	9.8	136	3.6	70
Watercress	0.1	43	120	0.2	41
Apples	0.03	6	4	0.10	1
Black currants	0.02	130	51	1.10	2
Oranges	0.11	59	43	0.10	1
Strawberries	0.0	58.8	16	0.40	1
Baked beans	0.09	0	53	1.40	530
Grilled Canadian bacon	0.8	0	10	0.8	1,546
Stewed beef	0.05	0	18	3.10	320
Canned sardines	0.04	0	550	2.90	650
Whole milk	0.03	1	115	0.06	55
Cheddar cheese	0.03	0	720	0.30	670
Low fat fruit yogurt	0.05	1	150	0.10	64
Chocolate	0.10	0	220	1.60	120
Chocolate cookies	0.03	0	110	1.70	160

Glossary

amino acid   chemical building block that makes up proteins

anemia   when a person does not have enough healthy red blood cells to keep his or her cells supplied with oxygen

antioxidant   substance that helps to neutralize the chemicals called free radicals, which can cause cancer and heart disease

artery   tube that carries blood from the heart to different parts of the body

bacteria   single, living cells. Most types of bacteria are harmless, but some types can cause disease.

bile   green liquid made in the liver that breaks up the fats in food

birth defect   physical problem or condition that is present when a baby is born

bone marrow   jelly-like substance in the center of some bones. Red and white blood cells are manufactured in the bone marrow.

carbohydrate   substance in food that your body uses to provide energy. Foods that contain carbohydrates include bread, rice, potatoes, and sugar.

carbon dioxide   one of the gases in air. Animals breathe out carbon dioxide.

cell   smallest living unit. The body is made up of many different types of cells, such as bone cells, blood cells, and skin cells.

chemical change   joining of two substances to produce a different substance, or the splitting up of a substance into two or more different substances

chemical reaction   process that occurs when substances undergo chemical change

cholesterol   fatty substance found in some foods and in most parts of your body, including the blood

chyme   mushy liquid that passes from the stomach to the small intestine. It is formed from partly digested food mixed with the digestive juices of the stomach.

compound   substance made up of two or more simple substances

dentin   thick bone-like tissue that makes up most of a tooth

diarrhea   when the feces are loose and watery

digestive system   organs of the body that are used to digest food

dissolve   when a solid or gas merges with a liquid

DNA   substance that genes are made from. DNA carries the genetic information that makes you a unique individual.

duodenum first part of the small intestine

eczema skin disorder that causes patches of very dry, itchy skin and small red pimples

element simple substance made up of only one type of chemical

energy ability to do work or to make something happen

enzyme substance that helps a chemical change take place faster without being changed itself

esophagus tube through which food travels from the mouth to the stomach

fat substance in some foods that your body uses to provide energy. Fat is stored by your body in a layer below the skin and helps to keep you warm.

fatty acid type of acid found in animal fat and vegetable oils and fats

fiber in food, the undigested parts of plants

free radical chemical that can cause cancer and heart disease

genetic code instructions that tell your cells what to do and how to make new cells

hemoglobin chemical in your red blood cells that carries oxygen

hormone substance produced by different parts of the body that affects or controls particular organs, cells, or tissues

immune system body's defenses against germs and diseases

infectious easily spread from one person to another

large intestine part of the intestines through which undigested food passes after it has left the small intestine

metabolic rate speed at which your body's chemical reactions occur

molecule smallest part of a substance that can exist and still be that substance

nervous system series of connected nerves throughout the body

nutrient part of food that your body needs to get energy, to build and repair cells, and for the cells to function properly. Nutrients include carbohydrates, fats, proteins, vitamins, and minerals.

organ part of the body with a specific function. An organ is made up of different types of tissue.

oxygen invisible gas that is one of the gases in air. The body needs oxygen in order to break down sugar to form energy.

pharynx back of the throat

premature happening too soon. A premature baby is one who is born before he or she is due.

protein complex chemical that the body needs to grow and repair cells

puberty age when the body begins to produce sex hormones and becomes able to reproduce sexually

saliva watery liquid made by glands in the mouth and the inside of the cheeks

small intestine   part of the intestine into which food passes from the stomach to be digested and then absorbed into the blood. Undigested food passes through the small intestine into the large intestine.

soluble   able to dissolve in liquid

spina bifida   inherited disease that affects the spine

starch   carbohydrates stored in plants

stress   strain or pressure

stroke   when a blood vessel in the brain bursts or is blocked by a clot of blood, damaging part of the brain

tissue   part of the body made up of the same type of cells

thyroid gland   gland that affects growth and the production of energy and waste in the body

trace element   mineral that is important for health but is only needed in very small quantities

virus   type of germ that causes certain diseases. Viruses are smaller than bacteria.

Find Out More

Books

Ballard, Carol. *Exploring the Human Body: The Stomach and Digestion.* Farmington Hills, Mich.: KidHaven, 2005.

Ballard, Carol. *Making Healthy Food Choices: Food for Feeling Healthy.* Chicago: Heinemann Library, 2007.

Parker, Steve. *Break It Down: The Digestive System.* Chicago: Raintree, 2007.

Websites

www.cnpp.usda.gov
This site from the Center for Nutrition Policy and Promotion, a part of the U.S. Department of Agriculture, provides information about health and nutrition. Included is the "MyPyramid" food pyramid, which offers guidelines for a healthy, balanced diet.

www.nutrition.gov
Learn more about nutrition at this educational site set up by the U.S. Department of Agriculture.

www.mckinley.uiuc.edu/Handouts/snacks_smart.html
Read about all types of healthy snacks.

Index